MW00477120

LOVE YE ONE ANOTHER

By

Lao Russell

A selection from
GOD WILL WORK <u>WITH</u> YOU
BUT NOT <u>FOR</u> YOU

A Living Philosophy

University of Science and Philosophy
Swannanoa, Waynesboro, Virginia 22980

Love Ye One Another
By
Lao Russell
1904-1988)

ISBN 1-879605-46-5

Edited by Emilia Lee Lombardi
Printed by Mid Valley Press

"Love ye one another all men,
for ye are one in Me.
Whatsoe'er ye do to one in Me
ye do to all, for all are one in Me.
Love thy brother as thy self.
Serve thy brother before thy self.
Lift high thy brother.
Lift him to high pinnacles,
For thy brother is thy self,"

— The Divine Iliad

PREFACE

The booklet you hold in your hand contains a penetrating description of the greatest force in the Universe. That force is Love, but most of the world perceives it in a limited, self-centered sense.

Walter Russell's illuminated insight into the nature of Man and Woman allowed him to explain rationally and scientifically their oneness with God.

Lao Russell, who devoted her life to extending this great Message to the world, wrote vividly of the false security so many of us find in our material prosperity and emotional indulgence.

They stressed that Love in its fullest sense was the natural driving force toward unity, the ultimate human impulse through which we come to recognize our connection with one another and with God.

Your appreciation of this basic principle of Creation will lead you to a new understanding of Love in action. It will teach you to recognize that the pain of others is your pain and that the gift you offer to those in need is the greatest gift you will ever receive.

Wishing you love and understanding,

Joseph B. Yount III
Chairman of the Board
University of Science and Philosophy

January 1996

There is a
destiny that
makes us brothers.
None goes his
way alone.
All that we send
into the lives
of others
Comes back into
our own.

by Edwin Markam

LOVE YE ONE ANOTHER

"He who giveth love prospereth mightily, but he who taketh aught gaineth naught."

The Divine Iliad

Love is the foundation of the world. All men are forever seeking it. They have forever been seeking it all down the ages — but man is still new. He does not yet know how to find the love and happiness he seeks. He gropes for the road to it, travels it a short way and then plunges into an abyss.

The dawn has not yet come to help man see the road or know how to find it. Once again he has traveled the road of life a short way and is again falling into another abyss of his own making. Man does not yet know how to live with other men. *He has not yet found that every other man on earth is a part of his very body, his very self, not merely his brother.*

No man would intentionally hurt his own body but he intentionally hurts other parts of his own body which he thinks of as other men, not knowing that they are one and inseparable from him. He knows that he cannot hurt any part of his own body without hurting all of it, but he has not yet found that he cannot hurt any man, anywhere, without hurting himself and every man, everywhere. He has only partly become aware that every happening anywhere, happens everywhere. Yes, he knows that, but he thinks only of the human voice in that connection. The radio is familiar to him. He hears the voice of the news reporter telling of the anguish in Saigon or Korea. He also hears of the tortured in concentration camps, and of hundreds of sons of the world mothers buried alive by their own other selves. They do not even know that they are also burying themselves and all mankind. Man does not yet know that the anguish of the homeless in Saigon is world anguish, not just for Saigon alone. Those homeless, barefoot mothers, carrying naked and hungry babies are not only walking from their burning homes into their own city; they are walking into your own doorway.

It Can Happen Here

How many thousands of people in Europe have read of atrocities in other European countries, as you read of them here, and have thought, as you think, that "it could not happen here," only to find that it has happened there. We have comfortable homes, a car and every necessity of life. So had they, but there were those who *"know not what they do,"* who stepped into factories and homes and ordered them out with nothing but the clothing on their backs.

Three thousand miles away means nothing. What happens three thousand miles away happens in our own homes. People who are hurt three thousand miles away are being hurt in our own homes, for what happens anywhere happens everywhere. Thousands of our own sons died while the people of Korea, nine thousand miles away, were being hurt. Their hurt was every man's hurt. When one part of the world is suffering untold agonies and our part of the world boasts of great and increasing prosperity, as we are now doing, we are living in a fool's paradise. Those untold sufferings of the other half of the world are debits which must be deducted from our credits to make us poorer each year instead of richer.

No country can call itself "richer" when it profits itself by another nation's poverty. Our riches of today are the fruits of world crime. They always have been. This has always been a gangster world which enriches itself by impoverishing others. No gangster has ever been able to hold what he has stolen and live in peace without having armored cars and body-guards to help him try to hold it. For such a man to call himself rich, prosperous, and happy because of his mighty possessions is living in the fool's paradise that our world is living in. Never in history has this man-made gangster world ever had to have so many armored cars, and so huge a bodyguard, to protect itself and its mighty possessions from further confiscation by greater gangsters.

War To End Wars?

Only one decade ago we ended a second war which we had fought to end wars. We looked for an era of peace, but instead of that we have spent many more billions to protect ourselves from more enemies that our unbalanced civilization has been perpetually making for ages. Shall we again have to fight another war to end wars? If so, will it end them? Has war ever ended in peace and happiness without leaving an accumulation of fear, hatred and enmity to breed more wars?

Yes, we know that it is necessary — and expedient — but what kind of world is it that makes such an expedient become a necessity? Where is the wisdom of building that kind of world by people whose sole desire in life is to find happiness, peace and prosperity? ***"Man always kills the thing he loves,"*** and that is what he has done again and what he must pay for. The game of seesaw, which life is, cannot be played very long with a full-grown man on one end of it and a little girl on the other end. Nor can our civilization continue the game for very long with an elephant on one end and an ant on the other, as it is so hysterically trying to do.

Start All Over Again

Again I say that the only hope for saving this unhappy, unbalanced world of fear is to start all over again and make a new world which has in it the aggressive and forceful character of the male, equally balanced by the restraining spiritual force of the female which directs the male force into **constructive** instead of **destructive** directions. We may as well do this and not continue in the old self-suicidal way, for Natural Law will not permit such unbalance to continue.

It is time that we looked at the falsity of the riches we boast about and realize that our country is poorer today than it has ever been in history. This once bountifully solvent nation is insolvent today. Its debts are greater than the real estate values of the whole country. Every child who has been born since 1950 is many thousands of dollars in debt at birth, with no assets to pay that debt, and no hope of getting out of debt during his whole life. Not one man in this country owns his own home, because it is first security for a national debt, thus making every citizen insolvent. That is why our so-called prosperity has no foundation, for we have made our nation prosperous by making its people insolvent.

It HAS Happened Here

Do not, therefore, say that "it cannot happen here," when it has already happened here. Do not also say that we are rich and prosperous because everyone is earning money by taking it from his own pocket to fill another pocket of his own. Do not be so sure for even what you think you have may not be yours tomorrow.

When the world talks prosperity because we have sold a million more automobiles this year than last, and the stock market is higher than ever before in history, that is but one side of the world ledger. The other side of the world ledger, however, tells us that there is a corresponding increase in crimes, criminals and youth delinquents. Also that there are billions and billions being spent to protect us from our enemies in order that we may even survive to do business. Thousands of American lives are being sacrificed to protect us from enemies which we made by business greed.

These tragic items are our fixed overhead charges which enable us to build our seeming prosperity. Where, then, are the profits?

What people fail to realize is that seeming world prosperity will not save a falling civilization. The Babylonian, Greek and Roman civilizations were luxuriously wealthy when they fell. Too much luxury even contributed to the fall of civilizations just as money and luxury in a home often degenerate progressive families into what are known as the idle rich.

Moral Degeneracy Alone Destroys

Moral degeneracy alone destroys civilizations. Money or prosperity is not a controlling factor. Even if we sell fifty million more cars this year than last, or even if stocks sell for five times as much this year as last, this civilization will as surely fall as other morally decadent civilizations have fallen unless the *cause* of its falling is removed. One might as consistently tell a man who has a very bad heart that nothing can happen to him because his business is doubling its profits yearly.

Why is all this? We do not know how to live. We place money values even ahead of life itself. We do not know the value of our neighbor to ourselves. We do not even know the relationship of our neighbor to ourselves. We have no living philosophy to live by; we have but a philosophy to die by. That philosophy is based upon disunity, separateness and greed. That is what I mean by the philosophy of death. It means that you cannot live by it. *A living philosophy must be based upon unity - oneness — inseparability -- and interdependence.* It must have **love** as its motive instead of **fear.** It must see the good in man and not look upon him as sinful and evil. *The world becomes what the world thinks.* It thinks of man as sinful and evil and he has become what his own thoughts have made him. He has made a world of hate and fear, and where hate is love cannot also be.

One Family

There will come a time, however, when the whole human race will know itself as one family, with but the one FATHER-MOTHER of all. When that day comes, every man will be the father and mother, or brother and sister, or son and daughter of every other man. As love comes into the world with spiritual unfolding, separateness and disunity go out of it. With love comes knowledge of the power of unity which makes the power of every man become the power of every other man. Separateness makes one man want for himself what every other man also wants for himself. Separateness takes. It never gives, and long ages of taking must pass before he learns that *what he takes he never has, but what he gives he always has.*

The long ages will pass, however, and every man will serve every other man whom he knows as his very Self. Blood relationship is mighty in its desire to serve sons and daughters, or brothers and sisters, and fathers and mothers in one separate family. No matter what wrong a son may do to the whole world, the love of parents is greater than the fault.

The happy, peaceful and progressive home is one where each member of the family thinks first of each other member, serves *first* each other before himself, and freely gives without motive of self-gain. In the ideal family everyone will not only serve each other to make him happy but will refrain from doing anything to make any member of it unhappy. That is the ideal. That is what every home needs to make complete happiness for every member of it.

The world is one family of one world-home. The ideal world is one in which every member of it serves each other lovingly to give him happiness, and refrains from doing anything which will take his happiness away from him. That is the ultimate goal. That is what mankind is striving for. That is what he has been striving for over the long aeons. For these long ages he has ever been searching for the road which will lead to that goal of romance and peace.

The Ideal

Yes, that is the ideal — and the goal — but how very far the world-family is from such a goal! And how far the average individual family is away from it. It would be difficult to find such a family anywhere, but there are many of them who have so nearly approached it that their example is a light shining out of the darkness.

As for the world-family, that ideal is still so far away that it may again destroy itself several times before it learns its lesson sufficiently to function as a whole. If you know any family in your town whose members are as divided against each other as our present world-family is, you know for a certainty that such a family will break apart and go to pieces. You would know that its disunity would destroy it eventually. It would seem that the world-family has not even found the road which leads to unity and cohesiveness as yet.

Oh, how many individuals and families have thought that they have found the road to happiness and have lost it in just not knowing how to live it. *We have never really known how to live life, either individually or collectively, as families, cities or nations.* Life is an experiment in trying to find a way of life. It is full of the comedies, tragedies and other problems which confront everyone all of the time. They are always here, in your home and mine, in your life and mine. *And the greatest problems are how to meet them and dissolve them.*

A Living Philosophy

To have a living philosophy which will meet all problems alike and rise above them with glory rather than anguish, and become strong because of them, is of first import in man's self-education. Problems are all alike in principle. They differ only in details and form, like the ten thousand stories written around the same motive, so let us take a familiar one which thousands of men and women are facing in this immature civilization which is, as yet, but coming out of the dark.

A very happy woman was sure she had found romance, love, peace and security. Then one day her whole world crumbled and fell at her feet. Her husband telephoned her that he would be detained at the office until late. He had telephoned her a hundred times before saying he would be detained and she had never known a moment's concern, for she had known in her heart that it was all right. This time it was different. She trembled with some dread fear, even before lifting the receiver. His voice was the same cheerful voice but there was something strangely different about it. She was deeply disturbed, for some bits of gossip had reached her ears which she had ignored, but intuition was making it difficult to answer with the naturalness of her own cheerful voice.

For a long time she sat in silence by the telephone after hanging up the receiver. Something which had never entered that home before came into it at that moment. That which entered her home that night was the dread destroyer of all that man calls good in man's world. Its name is *tension.* Tension came into her home, her heart and her romance, to multiply until happiness became impossible for one who did not know how to meet it in any other way than tears, weepings, supplications and compromise.

When such a tragedy threatens the happiness of any woman or man, the event itself is of far less importance than the way one meets it. How will this particular woman meet it? That is what is important. As we are seeking a right way of life, and as life is full of big and little problems, let us take this particular problem of this grief-stricken woman and discuss the merits and philosophy from the point of view of Natural Law and God's ways and processes.

Two Ways of Meeting Problems

There are two ways of meeting every problem of life. This grief-stricken woman has her choice of those two ways. One way is the way of weakness, of tears, grief, pleadings and supplications. *That is the wrong way. It multiplies tensions by compromising. It attempts to cure wrong with wrong.* That is the weak way which creates a long life of continuous unhappiness. The strong way is by not compromising and knowing how to intelligently meet such a challenge. The weak way begins with multiplying tensions instead of dissolving them. That is the first thing that anyone should think of in meeting any problem. Whatever tension has been created by the appearance of that problem must be dissolved. It must be utterly eliminated, no matter what price must be paid in humility and material loss. Tensions cannot exist in anyone's life without his permission, nor without nourishment supplied by him. *Happiness and tension cannot possibly co-exist.*

A few agonizing weeks pass and this woman, whom we will call Sarah, has become quite convinced that another woman has come between herself and her husband. Being no longer able to stand the grief of it alone, she takes her first wrong step. Instead of working in the direction of dissolving the existent tension, Sarah tells her mother all about it. There are tears and much grief. Her mother is sorrowful and sympathetic. She shares her daughter's trouble with her. They cry a little together. Sarah thinks she feels a little better by feeling her mother's love and sympathy but what has really happened is that Sarah has created another tension and another problem.

Tensions cannot create happiness. They destroy it. Unintentionally Sarah took happiness away from her mother for herself but found only an increased tension and another problem. Two people now have a tension instead of one and the problem is doubled by the fact that the mother will either do something about it herself or advise Sarah to do something about it which Sarah should not do.

Seek Advice From God

Weak people always seek the advice of others. Strong people never do. Strong people may seek information but their decisions are their own. We tell our students that the only one to ever ask advice from is God. When you have a decision to make, go into your place of quiet, in your own room or out in the woods, or down by the sea, anywhere, where you can be all alone with God. *He will always give you the right answer. You already have the right answer within you. God will but awaken you to a realization of that fact.* Talk to God as you would talk to one you know whom you can love and trust beyond all others.

That is what Sarah should have done instead of complexing her problem by going to her mother. One cannot shift one's mental burden to another for each man's problem is his alone. When the burden of Sarah's problem was given to her mother instead of facing and solving it herself, the problem had doubled itself. Two now had it instead of one. Soon four had it, for Sarah's mother told Sarah's father and he consulted a lawyer. They all talked, and the town heard of it, and the gossips spread it. By the time Sarah had decided to talk to her husband, he had decided that the only right thing he could do was to get a divorce.

The happy ending which could have been possible was rendered impossible by the mere multiplication of one tension into a hundred. What he might have said to her alone, where he could open his heart to her, might have cured her heartache and saved their home. They could have both counted it as one of those human experiences that all people at some time encounter in their lives, which enrich one's life if conquered, but impoverish it if the experience is the conqueror.

When Sarah talked with her husband, her mother was with her to protest, to condemn and blame, and her father and lawyer were there to build an impenetrable wall around the case to keep peace and happiness out of it. Love knocked hard on the doors of that wall in the hope of being allowed to come in where the light of his love could be seen in his eyes and felt in their hearts. The words of the mother locked the doors still tighter and the formality of the father and lawyer made love stop knocking at the door to weep instead.

Thus it was that one more home was broken up. A problem of life — just one of the thousands of problems of life which will forever confront you, and me, and everyone who lives — succeeded in becoming real instead of its unreality being dissolved as black clouds dissolve to let the light come through.

That is what came of meeting that problem the wrong way, the weak way of self-injury, the way of tears, and grief, and a bid for sympathy, compassion and pity.

Dissolve Mental Tension

Had Sarah been a very strong woman and met her problem the way it should have been met from the first moment that she became aware of it, the very first thing she would do would be to dissolve that mental tension which the shock of discovery caused in her. *The strong person is one who learns to take all things alike without affecting that inner ecstasy for long, which gives one strength.* That high state of happiness is the spiritual in one which so far transcends any human emotions that nothing can touch one beyond a passing moment. Such a person can find balance speedily, no matter what tension comes into his life to disturb its balance.

I know a strong man whose heart was so full of the rhythms of the singing of all Nature that he was able to continue the farce of matrimony, in name-only existence, for many, many years, as mere background for his picture of life. He could at all times walk away into the woods with a biscuit in his pocket and spend a day in ecstasy of Mind. His sketchbook recorded the beauty of motives for nocturnes and symphonies, or perhaps the graceful branches and great tree trunks which held them up into the high heavens, and told of his all-day loving communion with them and their Creator. He thus immunized himself from even the possibility of a disturbing tension.

When serious tensions arise between man and wife they should first talk to God about them. A natural state of happiness must first be restored. When one talks to God about any trouble on the waters of life, they become calm and still, and one who knows the ecstasy of the kingdom of heaven within one's Self finds that heaven, and knows that nothing on earth can hurt one unless one accepts the hurt. *Good thoughts dissolve unpleasant ones.*

When calm has been restored, then is the time to sit down quietly together and face the cause of the original tension. From such a discussion both parties will often discover that both have unknowingly contributed to the rift. Perhaps either one or the other has felt a lack of romance and sought it from another. When these marital differences are faced together alone — without multiplying tensions by outside advice and interferences — they can usually be dissolved and good can come from them. There are very few who can possibly pass through life without having experiences which they deeply regret, but with knowledge they can strengthen their character and immunize themselves from a repetition of the same or more serious ones. ***Thus good can come from an experience which could also destroy one.***

The One Motive of Love

People in all the world forever seek love, but few find it for very few know where to seek it or how to find it. And many shut it out from themselves because the love they seek must fit within a motive, or pattern, which they have created for the use of love. He who seeks love with a personal motive behind it will never find it. If money, or personal support, or social position is the motive, they may find what they seek but they will not have found love. Like the man who seeks happiness through money, he may find the money but not the happiness he sought.

Love can have but one motive — to give out from itself in order to find unity. The greatest urge in all Nature is UNITY.

This quality in Nature is so little understood, and so rarely practiced as a consequence, that it must be dwelt upon and made clear. Unity means the ending of separateness, or division, or multiplication, or difference of opinion, or anything whatsoever which can be said to be two. Unity means complete ONENESS.

Separateness is in itself the quality of tension. Every state of motion in the universe is exerted either for creating tensions or eliminating them.

A man who deeply desires money must use much effort to obtain it. That effort creates a tension. When he has obtained all he wants and locks it up to keep it for himself, he does not realize that he has locked up the tension of accumulating it. He no longer has the money he sought for the purpose of giving him happiness. He has but the tension of worry and strain of keeping it. He must watch it lest thieves take it from him.

Give Love and Happiness

To thus lock one's happiness in a box, as Scrooge did, means that he is without happiness, as Scrooge was. The moment he gives love and happiness out to one who needs it, love and happiness will be regiven to him. He then has what he has given, but never can have while it is locked in a box for himself alone.

Even this example must be amplified, for very many people do not understand what Jesus meant when he told the rich man to go and sell all he had and give it to the poor.

I once heard a rich man combat that idea severely. He argued that if he sold all he had and gave a million dollars to the poor he would himself be poor, and those to whom he gave his million would also be as poor the next day.

That would be only giving money to people who wanted only money and had no way of regiving money, I explained, but if you gave love with the money by giving it out of yourself, they would then have a way of regiving both the love and the money. In such a way of giving, you never could be poor for you could never give it without a balancing regiving.

Suppose that there were five hundred poor and needy families in your town. Instead of dividing your million dollars with them in money, you bought a textile industry and divided that up with them to give permanent employment to all of them, they would then have the happiness of permanent security which they would regive to you in love. And you would have the happiness of giving them the love which they needed. And the million dollars should soon be two million which they also would regive to you.

That is what Jesus meant when He said "all you have." He did not mean money alone. He also meant the love you had in you to give which money made possible, but the love was not in the money; it was in the man. The money without the love is worthless.

When a man thus gives himself "to the poor," as well as giving his money, he finds unity through action, which Nature demands to complete her transactions. Otherwise, he would merely have been giving only charity which is not in conformity with Nature's law. Nature demands that everything given be equally regiven.

Self-Created Tensions Destroy Happiness

Self-created tensions which destroy the happiness of many families have numerous illustrations in homes where mothers and fathers prevent their children from living normal lives by insisting upon living their lives for them.

A very happy home of father, mother, daughter and son lived together in great harmony until both children became old enough to court, and be courted. The father died and the mother suddenly developed the idea that her children should sacrifice their lives for her. Instead of the natural desire of wanting to see her children happily married, the thought of losing them struck terror in her heart. Since losing her husband she felt that their sole purpose henceforth was to take their father's place in her affections and support. She had to fall back on her old occupation of dressmaking to support them until both children were able to work and support her.

Tensions began when Susan's first beau came to spend an evening with her in her home. Her mother strongly resented this first serious threat to her happiness. Susan was told that she was not old enough to think of such things. She also had her mother to consider and could not waste time on boys. The mother sat through the young man's first visit, and the second, but a third visit did not take place. The boy sought other and more pleasant fields. Love had not ripened in him far enough to make a fight for love against such resistance. Young love must have suitable soil to grow in just as a young plant must also have suitable soil to grow in.

Dick also spent evenings with different girls and went to many parties, but when he seemed to prefer one certain girl his mother reminded him that he was not to think of such things while she needed his love and support. She so imbued both children with that idea that they gradually came to believe it. Year by year went by in this same manner. Each of them felt their mother's possessiveness. She constantly

reminded them of her years of self-sacrifice —
years she had given for them — and of their
first duty to their mother. From the moment
that the mother's assertion of possession of her
children began, happiness flew out of the win-
dow of that home. The **first tension began at
that moment.** As tension multiplied its poten-
tial, happiness divided it. When tensions grow
strong enough in families, something snaps.

Susan had grown to be thirty-four and Dick
thirty-six. Susan had been put on the hopeless
list by suitors for a long time. She had received
hardly any attention for years. Then something happened. A boy whom she deeply
loved and wanted to marry when she was
twenty-six, who had left at that time to take a
position in another town, returned home. A
great surge of suppressed happiness came to
Susan followed by a deeper surge of tears
when she thought of her duty to her mother,
which had been so indelibly instilled in her.
Her suitor would not take "no" for an answer,
saying: "Your mother has already taken ten

years of happiness away from us. She is an unnatural mother and I shall tell her so. You can contribute your share to her support, as usual, but you are going to marry me and that's the end of that."

There was a scene, a memorable scene, but something snapped in Dick, too, and he said things to his mother that he never dreamed possible, so hypnotized had he been by the idea that sacrifice for his mother was his un-questionable duty. When he found that the assurance of continued support meant so little to her in comparison with the desire to possess her children, he said to her:

"Mother, you have had your marital happi-ness, you have had a husband and children and a home. It is not you who have sacrificed for us. You have sacrificed us for you. Susan loves John and should have married him ten years ago. She will marry him now and I will marry Nancy who is growing old waiting for me. You should find happiness in your added children and grandchildren, as other mothers do. I hope you will, too, but we have finally awakened to the truth of the situation and shall live our normal lives as you lived yours."

This particular mother was unable to adjust herself to the naturalness of family growth because she had never learned to give happiness by sharing. She was unable to find happiness in the midst of an abundance of it. Therefore she manufactured her own loneliness and unhappiness. Thus one more home in which were all the elements for making happiness was broken up by *not knowing how to live life in harmony with the one law of balance which governs all life.* This was just one more problem of the many thousands of problems which everyone meets continuously. There should be no difficulty in meeting any one of them if people have unfolded far enough spiritually to first ask God to tell them how to settle their problems.

The Right Way Is The Only Way

The law courts are jammed with thousands of human problems which need not be there. Every man who sues another man knows in his heart what is the right thing for him to do, and the man who is sued also knows what is the right thing for him to do. Both knowing that, and knowing that the right way is the only way, why do they still fight each other in court, like enemies, instead of sitting down together as friends? The answer is that the majority of people who go to law courts with their economic difficulties either want to get the best of the other fellow and get all they can for themselves or dodge a responsibility which they know they should meet. By defending an action, they hope to dodge much more of that responsibility than by paying it in full.

One of our lawyer students said that fully seventy percent of our economic problems could be settled out of court if people really wanted to be fair. He has caused many of his clients to sit face to face with their opponents and settle their differences on a fair basis which keeps friendships instead of on a forced basis which loses friendships. He cited a case where his client's opponent refused to meet in a friendly way to discuss a suit for heavy damages, which his opponent insisted upon instituting. This lawyer and his client had concluded that a generously fair amount due to the opponent was fifty thousand dollars and had offered that amount in a friendly communication.

The offer was refused and the suit for $200,000 went into court which awarded only $20,000 instead of $200,000 on the ground of contributory negligence on the part of the plaintiff. When the client said to his attorney: "Well, John, we have saved $30,000 by going to law," the attorney surprised him by replying: "No, we have not saved $30,000 for we are going to send him the $50,000 which we offered him."

"Why in the world do we do that? We won the case, did we not?" the client asked.

"Yes, we won it but we will lose it if we do not do what we thought in our hearts was fair to do. If the law gives him less than what we thought fair, we are hurting ourselves by taking advantage of it and losing a friend as well."

A check for $50,000 was sent with a letter which started with these words: "Dear John: I deeply regret the decision of the court in the case just settled. We may have disagreed between ourselves about the amount you were entitled to and that we should pay, but our conclusion that we fairly owed you the amount of our enclosed check cannot be altered by even a court decision, which we are unwilling to accept as fair."

It is needless to say that such a conclusion canceled out a tension which might never have been canceled out in the lifetime of those two men. Had the check for $20,000 been sent to the plaintiff's attorney through the attorney for the defendant, there would be a residual tension accompanying that check which might have cost ten times the $30,000 saved in good will.

The combativeness of human nature disappears entirely when the love force of Nature destroys separateness and its consequent selfishness. Combativeness and selfish desires of getting all that one can out of a transaction with another man is an attempt to bargain with God. That is impossible. God will not let you take more than the law or less than the law. If you force a settlement with your neighbor for less than Nature's **one law of balance** should give you, there will come with it a costly tension which can never be canceled

Man Works Against Great Tensions

To better comprehend the permanent damage of a tension which always lasts until canceled, take a strong piece of rubber and stretch it as far as you can and hold it there. Not for one second can you be unaware of that straining tension which you have made for yourself. If you were obliged to hold it in that position, you would give all you had to be freed from it. Try also to do your daily tasks while leaning even three degrees from your equally balanced position. Just that little three degrees would make your life many times more difficult and uncomfortable, yet practically every man on earth is in that position, or worse.

Every man has a certain number of tensions that he has created in his daily life which he must continually work against. Added to that is a great world tension of unknown power which everyone knows could destroy half the world overnight. That great world tension exists. No one knows exactly what it is but everyone feels an ominous threat of an unknown something in the air which prevents complete happiness. Wherever tensions exist anywhere, complete happiness is impossible. That is why every problem which comes into anyone's life should be faced immediately, no matter what it is, and eliminated. Search for the *cause* of it. You probably made it in some dealing during the day. If you are disturbed about it, that means that there is a residual unbalance in it that you have not canceled. You cannot possibly be completely happy until you have voided that residual unbalance. It is as though it is making you lean several degrees off center from gravity.

A renowned New York industrialist, who attributes his success to fair dealing and giving service instead of taking it, said that if he found that he had hurt a friend he would seek him out at once and heal his hurt before the day could pass. That is such a simple principle to understand that it is strange that people do not realize it. Many a marriage could be saved if before going to sleep either the husband or wife said "I love you," after there had been a discordant note which left even a slight tension..

Loneliness

Consider the common problem of loneliness in a world where everyone is seeking friendships. Every lonely person is surrounded by love and friendship which is hers, or his, for the asking. They want to take it in instead of giving it out. They want attention to be shown to them instead of giving service to others. They wait for it to be given to them without giving anything out to others. Everyone who wants love and companionship can have it in abundance if they will only give loving friendship to everyone they meet. One cannot keep love away from one's self if one gives love. The girl who radiates friendliness and charm of manner attracts many more friends than the haughty self-centered one who demands admiration for herself.

Laotzu once said: ***"He who desires honors should first honor others."*** One who desires admiration must, therefore, first give admiration or forever be without it.

It matters not what your trouble or problem may be if you will but realize that God has forever whispered His loving instructions to you since your very beginning. God works with all of His creations all of the time. When, after long ages, men become aware of it, their very destinies are simplified by learning how to work with Him. Do not, therefore, wait until you go to bed to make your habitual prayer to Him. Be aware of His presence within you every moment, so that you are as aware that He is working with you as you are aware that your partner is working with you.

Unfolding Your Destiny

Moment-to-moment awareness of God's presence is needed for unfolding your destiny through work, and it is also needed to retain a state of perpetual inner joyousness which will immunize you from the toxins of fatigue. Joyousness is love. One whose nature is joyous will very often not show the slightest signs of fatigue, while the morose one, or one who does not love the work he is doing, will fatigue very quickly.

Again I say, life is difficult to live when one does not know the kingdom of heaven which centers him. The more that anyone acquires conscious awareness of God's eternal presence within him, the easier the living of life becomes.

This booklet closes with the admonishment to **"Love Ye One Another,"** as it opened with those same words, and as every chapter of life's experiences should begin and end,

—————————— for ——————————

Love is the foundation of Life.

———————————————————————

* * *

That which you do to others
you do to yourself.

Factual interpretation
of The Golden Rule

Every action in Nature is simultaneously
balanced by an equal reaction.

Scientific interpretation
of The Golden Rule

He who would command his destiny
must first learn how to balance
the conditions which control it.

The First Rule of Life

The law of equal giving for regiving is absolute. You must give equally for what is given you. An effort on your part must pay for the effort on God's part. *If you stop giving, you will shut off your own supply.* If the heavens cease giving rains to earth, the earth ceases giving crops and forests to the heavens.

* * *

God's law will never give you anything without an equivalent repayment in action. You must

nurture the health which is given
you and give much care to your
body as long as you use that gift.
You could starve with food ten feet
away from you unless you gave
effort to reaching for it and more
effort to preparing it for use.

* * *

*Love means exchange of service for
service—and God's law demands
that service given must equal
service rendered.*

WALTER RUSSELL
Author of

The Secret of Light
The Message of the Divine Iliad - Vol. I
The Message of the Divine Iliad - Vol. II
A New Concept of the Universe
The Secret of Working Knowingly With God
The Electric Nature of the Universe
Genius Inherent in Everyone
The Fifth Kingdom Man
The Dawn of a New Day in Human Relations
The Immortality of Man

WALTER and LAO RUSSELL
Co-Authors of

Home Study Course in *Universal Law, Natural Science
and Living Philosophy*
Scientific Answer to Human Relations
Atomic Suicide?
The World Crisis—Its Explanation and Solution
A Vision Fulfilled!

LAO RUSSELL
Author of

God Will Work <u>With</u> You But Not <u>For</u> You
Love—A Scientific & Living Philosophy of Love and Sex
Why You Cannot Die!—Reincarnation Explained

*For catalog on additional books and teachings by
Walter and Lao Russell, please write or phone:*

**The University of Science and Philosophy
Swannanoa, Waynesboro, Virginia 22980**
(540) 942-5161
(800) 882-LOVE (5683) Book Orders